CHICAGO PUBLIC LIBRARY
R01139 04206

D1161875

Penguins

by Louis Darling

William Morrow and Company New York 1956

Published simultaneously in the Dominion of
Canada by George J. McLeod Limited, Toronto.
Printed in the United States of America.
Library of Congress Catalog Card Number: 56-8790

Everything on the antarctic coast line is covered with snow and ice, except that here and there a black cliff, too steep to hold the snow, juts out of the sea. Ranges of white mountains disappear into the distance. Through the valleys glaciers make their slow, frozen way to the sea. The sea itself is frozen. It stretches northward in a white, jumbled expanse of ice. It is the middle of October, springtime in Antarctica, and the temperature has risen as high as zero. The sun, which had first shown itself after the long winter in late July, now stays in the sky for eighteen hours each day.

Way off in the distance, out on the frozen sea, there is another sign of spring. A line of small black dots is moving slowly toward the shore. The moving specks are penguins returning to the land of their birth. As in warmer lands, the coming of the birds is a sign of spring in this cold place. The penguins do not come on swift wings. They cannot fly, but plod slowly across the ice. They are coming for the same reason that brings all birds home in the springtime—to nest and mate and rear their young.

Usually only a few birds arrive at first. There are about forty in this bunch. As they reach the shore they seem to know very well where they are going. They scramble up the rocky cliffs, using wings, feet, and even bills to help them reach the windy places where the snow is thin. There they sit quietly by themselves or in little groups. The penguins are in fine condition, fat and sleek. Their backs are blue-black and their breasts snow-white. These are Adélie penguins, medium-sized as penguins go. They weigh ten pounds or so and stand about two feet high.

For twenty-four hours there are no more arrivals, but on the next day a long, wavy line appears out on the sea ice. There are hundreds and hundreds of birds. They amble along slowly. At times ten or twenty flop down on their chests and toboggan for a way, paddling

along with wings and feet. Then they walk upright again while another section of the line toboggans. The trip has been long. Their breath comes in wheezes. As they join the others on the shore there is a little calling and bickering, but mostly they lie or stand quietly.

The long line continues to wind across the ice for several days. There are thousands of penguins now. The colony is an uproar of squalling, fighting birds. Some have begun to scratch shallow scoops in the ground where the snow has melted away and their own warm breasts have thawed the soil. New birds are constantly arriving. The confusion and noise is so great that it is difficult to make out what happens to any one bird when it reaches the shore and throws itself into the struggle. There is no difference a human being can see between

any of them, male or female. But one particular penguin *is* different from the others. On his left leg is a numbered metal band. It was put there three years before at this same colony by a member of a group of scientists exploring and studying the antarctic. The scientist who placed the band on our penguin is a biologist. It was his job to study living things. By marking as many penguins as possible with his bands, he could keep track of individual birds and find out what they did from day to day and year to year.

The number on this penguin's band is eleven. If we look in the biologist's records we find the bird is a male that has mated and bred successfully for the last two years. He scrambles up the steep shore, paying no attention to the

crowds of noisy birds. Occasionally he dozes for a moment, then wakes and again climbs up through the colony. At last he walks up to a pair of penguins. One is sitting on a shallow scoop and the other is standing close by.

Number eleven stops in front of the sitting bird and lays an imaginary something he carries in his bill down close to it. He draws himself up to his full height, bill in air, and cackles loudly. Just then the standing bird lays a real pebble on the ground near the scoop. The sitting penguin looks at it, but does not touch it. Eleven stares at the standing bird and pecks it on the bill. The pecked one pecks back, and then lets fly with a wing, only to be whacked by Eleven with a rain of blows. The two penguins lean against each other and whale away furiously. The bird on the scoop becomes more and more excited. It rises and pecks first one, then the other of the battling pair. Only now

can it be seen that this bird, too, wears a metal band—number twenty. The record shows that she is a female and that for the last two years, as the mate of Eleven, she has nested on this same spot.

Suddenly one of the fighters turns and scuttles off into the milling crowd of the penguin colony. The second chases him a short way and then returns. The victor is Eleven. He picks up a pebble and lays it down again before Twenty, who has returned to her scoop. She carefully arranges it among a few others on the rim of the scoop. Then the pair stand upright, breast

to breast, and with open bills pointing up into the cold sky, necks swaying from side to side, they cackle wildly. Again and again they perform this strange ceremony, adding their shrill cries to the noise of all the thousands of penguins who have brought this lonely coast to life. Finally they settle down together side by side and seem to sleep.

After a time Eleven rises and peers about. He walks off, pauses behind a sitting bird, swiftly plucks a pebble from beneath it, and slips away into the throng. Soon Twenty and Eleven have built their scoop up with pebbles. Some of the little stones are stolen from neighbors and others are brought up from the beach. The work is hard, for unowned pebbles are scarce and Eleven and Twenty lose many of theirs when other birds steal them. The two penguins often go through their ceremony of display and occasionally, when one of them is alone, it draws itself up and gives a throbbing trumpet call. Then birds through the whole colony take up the trumpeting, and the lonely shores are filled with sound.

Never during this time have any of the birds gone back to the sea, although black water is now showing through leads in the sea ice.

The colony is almost full by the first of November. Greenish eggs are beginning to appear in some of the fifty thousand nests. The fighting, pairing, stealing, cackling, trumpeting, and confusion has gone on steadily night and day. The birds can be heard for miles. New pairs are formed from among the two-year-olds breeding for the first time, and birds who have lost their mates through death during the winter. A few pairs split up and mate with new partners. But, as a rule, a pair of last season reunites, even though each bird may arrive at the colony at a different time. Usually they return to the nesting site used the year before. A penguin will often "keep company" with a strange bird while waiting for its mate to return. But the true mate almost always wins the fight that takes place when this happens.

The nests are so close together on the favored high spots that the birds can touch each other. Continual fighting goes on all over the colony, fighting over mates, over pebbles, over nest sites, and just plain squabbling. It dies down a little as the eggs begin to appear. But fighting as well as play seems to be an important part of penguin social life and never stops.

During all this time the penguins have had no food. They live by absorbing the layer of fat that lies beneath their skin. This blubber, like that of seals, also protects them from the cold.

When two eggs are laid, the male takes over the job of keeping them warm and the female goes to sea to feed on the small crustaceans that make up a penguin's diet. Often she stays away for two weeks. This is as it should be, for the long fast and the task of producing the two eggs have put a great strain on her. Her weight has fallen from over twelve to under eight pounds. When she at last returns, the male leaves for about another two weeks. When he returns, the female again goes to sea, but for a shorter stay. By this time the chicks will probably be hatched.

The incubation time for an Adélie penguin egg is from four to five weeks, depending upon how well it is cared for. Penguin eggs have a rough time. It is a wonder that they ever hatch at all. The temperature often falls below zero and blizzards come, even in the summer. Often the nest and sometimes the sitting penguins are buried in snow. Water from melting snow floods many nests. Careless parents often kick eggs out of the nest, where they no longer recognize them. Hungry skua gulls, who breed nearby, are always ready to snatch eggs or chicks left unguarded for a moment. But the new lives inside the eggs are very tough, and enough do hatch every year to renew the population of millions of penguins.

When the chicks hatch, one parent fishes for them while the other guards and warms them. The pair share this work equally. The chicks weigh about three ounces when they are born. They are covered with dense, gray down. In four days they weigh twelve ounces and in twelve days two and one half pounds. They must grow to full size in seven or eight weeks, since summer is so short. The old birds are kept frantically busy catching enough food for themselves and bringing back the tremendous quantities needed for such growth. Penguins carry food to their young by swallowing it. When they reach the nest they disgorge it, and the little ones take it from their mouth or throat.

When one parent relieves another at the nest, they go through the same motions of neck weaving and cackling as during the nest-building and mating period. The bird returning from the sea comes to the nest without hesitation. It seems to recognize its mate from afar. They display loudly for a time, and then perhaps more quietly, uttering soft sounds with closed bills. When the sitting bird rises and the other takes its place, the noisy display starts all over again.

The young are old enough to leave the nest in about four weeks. Then they gather together in large gangs called créches. Here a few grown birds may stay with them while most of the parents go to sea to fish. The parents are able to find their own young in these groups and feed them.

Créches are doubtless formed as a protection for the chicks from the skuas, for the warmth to be gained by huddling together, and for the sociability that is so strong in penguins. Also the parents have more time to fish when one of them does not have to be constantly guarding the young.

When the chicks are first born, the parents do not know them from any of the others. Chicks can be switched from nest to nest, and the old birds will take over the strange babies without noticing that they are not their own. But by the time the créches are formed, the parents have learned to recognize their own young and will almost never feed a stranger. The chicks don't seem to know the parents so

well. They pester any bird that is returning with food. The adults are often followed all along the path from the sea by begging chicks. As the chicks grow, their piping little voices gradually change into a call which has much the same sound as the display cackle of the adults. They greet their parents with this call when they come with food, and when still older they also go through the display motions.

With all the work the old birds have to do, they still have time to play. They gather at the ice edge in noisy crowds. They run along and seem to dare each other to dive first. When one does plunge, the others follow like "shot poured out of a bottle." Then they pop up and frolic about in the water, splashing and cleaning themselves of the mud of the nesting ground. When they tire of play, they return to the colony and stand about in groups, chattering away to other birds. Often a bunch returning meet a group going to sea, join them, and go through the game all over again.

When the penguin chicks are grown to full size, they begin to shed their baby down. Underneath, pushing it off, grow the adult feathers. The chicks still have not entered the water and still have to be fed, although they are by now as big as their parents. When all the down is finally shed, the feeding is stopped. It is almost March and winter is near. All the Adélies must migrate into the great band of floating pack ice that encircles Antarctica. The chicks must learn to swim and fish by themselves. They are fearful of the water at first. But soon they are swimming with a skill that is born in them.

After the young have learned to fish, the adult birds shed their old worn plumage and grow new feathers. They stay on the land until the moult is finished. Then they move northward into the pack ice. Their going is a sign of winter, just as their coming was a sign of spring. The nights grow longer. By the middle of May the sun will no longer rise. Blizzards and deathly cold will hold the land until spring brings the penguins back to the rocky coast again.

There are seventeen species of penguins, most of which live in cold, distant places, far from the warmth of summer. The appearance and habits of all the species are quite similar. None of them can fly and all of them can swim like a fish. They are wonderfully able to find food and take care of themselves in the sea.

Most species breed on the lonely islands of the South Atlantic, South Pacific, and Indian Oceans, and feed in the cold waters around

GENTOO PENGUIN

RINGED PENGUIN

MAGELLAN PENGUIN

MACARONI PENGUIN

them. The Adélie and emperor penguins breed on the coasts of Antarctica. The great emperor penguin, the largest of them all, weighs as much as seventy pounds. Unlike all other penguins, it lays its eggs and rears its young during the dark months of the southern winter on the ice along the coasts of Antarctica, when temperatures fall as low as seventy degrees below zero and blizzards howl.

Emperor and king penguins do not build

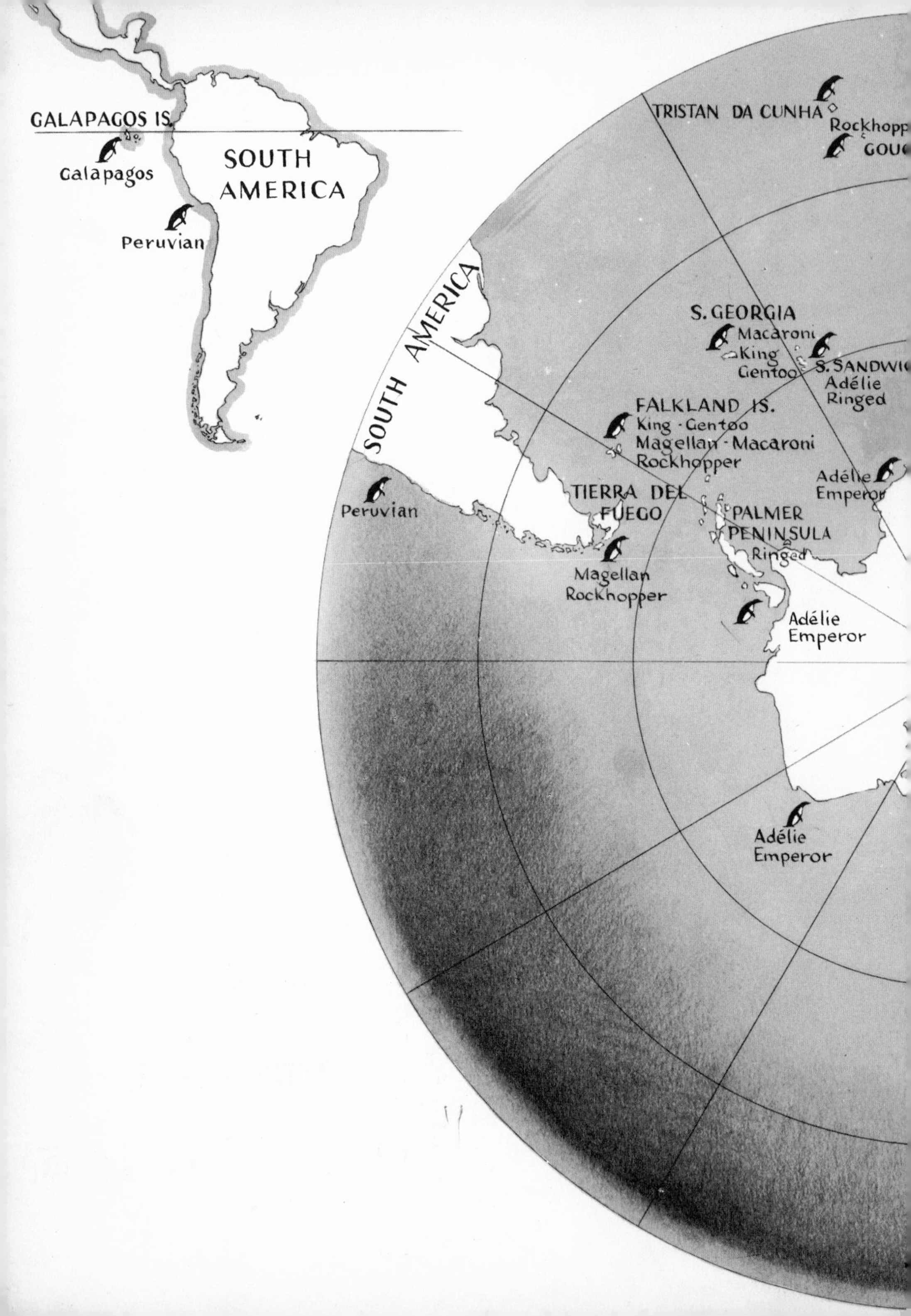

GALAPAGOS IS.
Galapagos
SOUTH AMERICA
Peruvian
TRISTAN DA CUNHA
Rockhopp
GOU
SOUTH AMERICA
S. GEORGIA
Macaroni
King
Gentoo
S. SANDWI
Adélie
Ringed
FALKLAND IS.
King · Gentoo
Magellan · Macaroni
Rockhopper
Adélie
Emperor
TIERRA DEL FUEGO
PALMER PENINSULA
Ringed
Peruvian
Magellan
Rockhopper
Adélie
Emperor
Adélie
Emperor

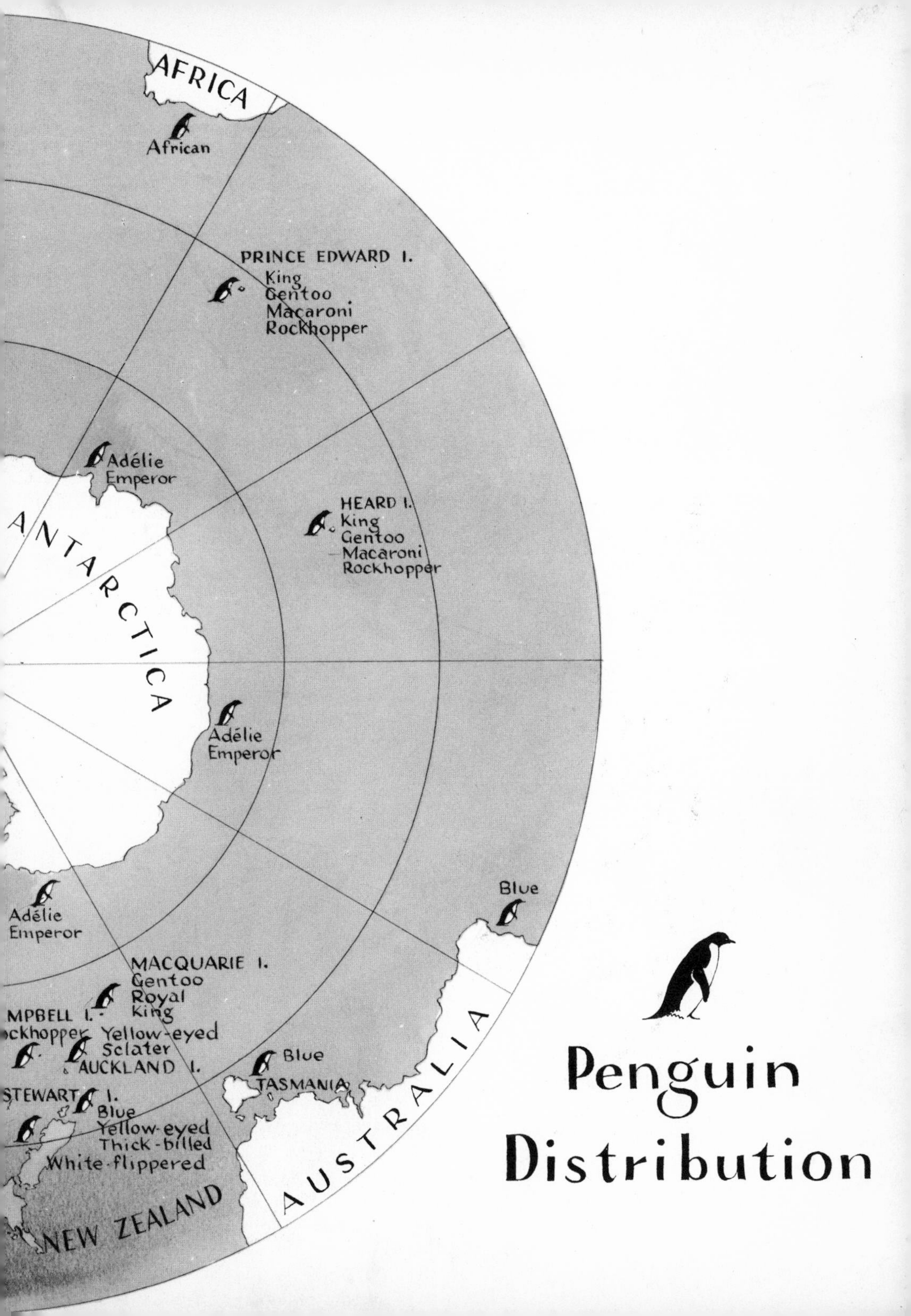

Penguin Distribution

nests at all, but brood their single egg on top of their feet, protected by a fold of skin in front and by the tail behind. Others, like the Adélies, dig scoops in the ground and line them with stones, bones, and sometimes moss and grass. Still others nest in burrows which they dig with their feet and bills.

Many penguin species live on islands farther north than the antarctic, where the climate is

EMPEROR PENGUIN

KING PENGUIN

warmer but the water still is cold. The little Galapagos penguin is the smallest species, weighing only four or five pounds. It lives the farthest north—on the Galapagos Islands, which are on the equator but are surrounded by the cold Humboldt current. There are no penguins in the northern hemisphere. The warm waters near the equator form a barrier which has kept these cold-water birds from spreading to northern seas.

GALAPAGOS PENGUINS

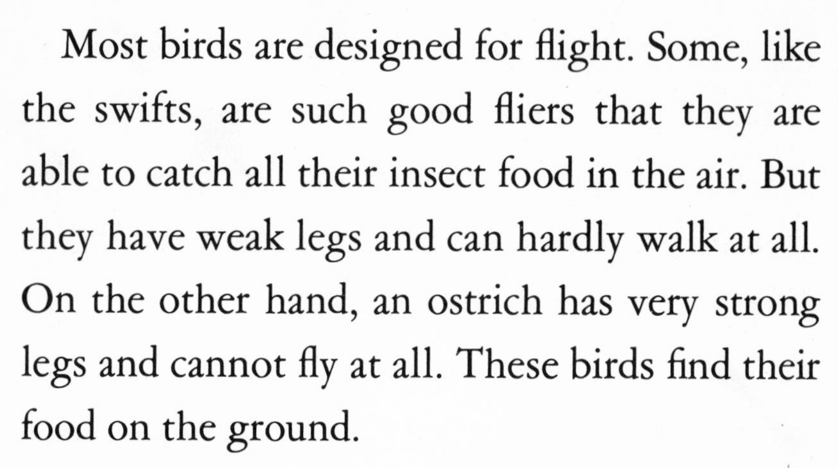

Most birds are designed for flight. Some, like the swifts, are such good fliers that they are able to catch all their insect food in the air. But they have weak legs and can hardly walk at all. On the other hand, an ostrich has very strong legs and cannot fly at all. These birds find their food on the ground.

Penguins get all their food from the sea and use their wings, not for flying, but as paddles for swimming. Many of them spend months at

sea without ever returning to the land at all.

Life in the water requires abilities that are not needed for life in the air or on land. The whole penguin, as well as its paddle wing, is different from other birds. The very things that make it possible for a bird to fly like a swift or run like an ostrich would handicap it in swimming. It is true that many birds can both swim and fly. But no bird who can fly can swim as well as a penguin.

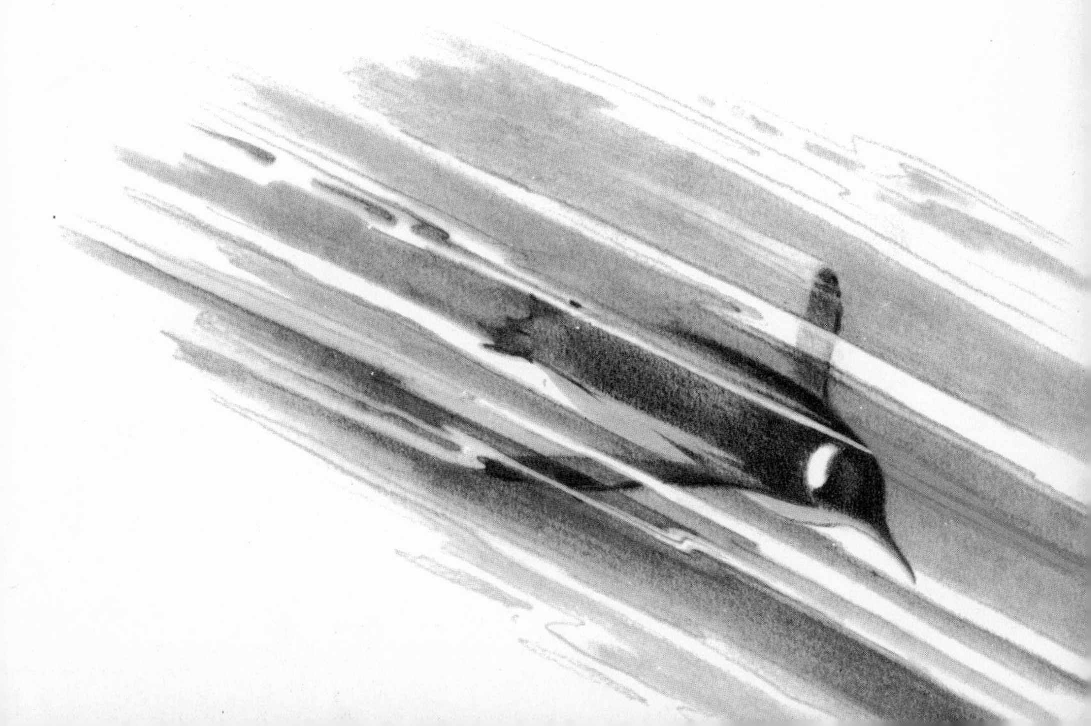

In spite of the fact that penguins live so differently from all other birds, they are still true birds, and have muscles, bones, and organs very much like those of flying birds. Because of this we know that the ancestors of penguins must have been able to fly. Probably, since they fed on the surface of the sea, they slowly lost the power of flight while gaining the power to

swim faster and dive deeper. This new ability opened up a huge area where birds could live without competing with other birds. Therefore the new kind of bird, the penguin, was successful. Of course this happened very slowly, millions of years ago. But by Miocene times, twenty-five million years ago, there were penguins very much like those now alive.

The feathers of most birds grow only from certain areas of the body called feather tracts. The bare spaces between these tracts do not show, since they are covered by nearby feathers. Penguin's feathers, which are very short, grow all over the bird in almost as regular a way as scales on a fish. They leave no bare spots unprotected from cold air and water.

A penguin's body feathers are small, with flattened shafts. They are quite downy at the base, but shiny near the tip. They lie close to

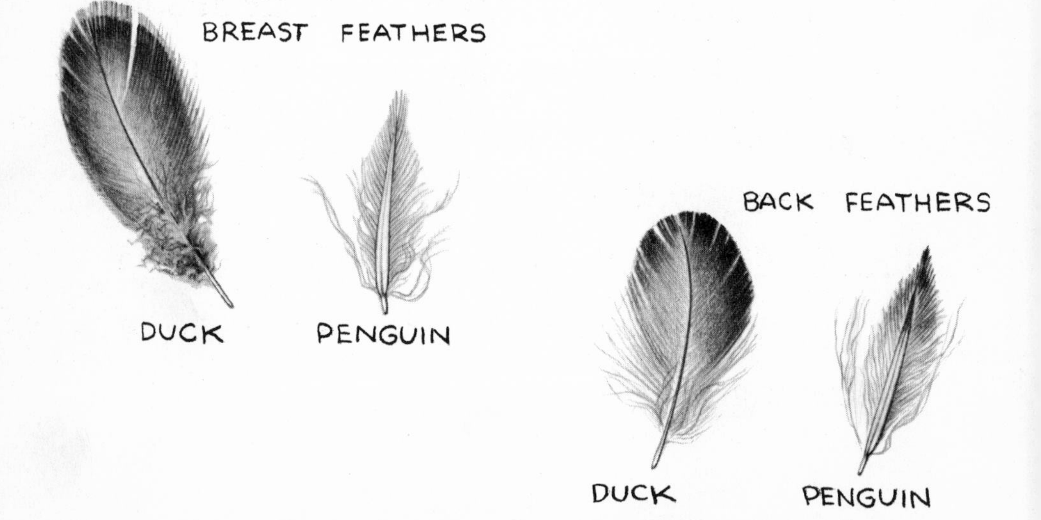

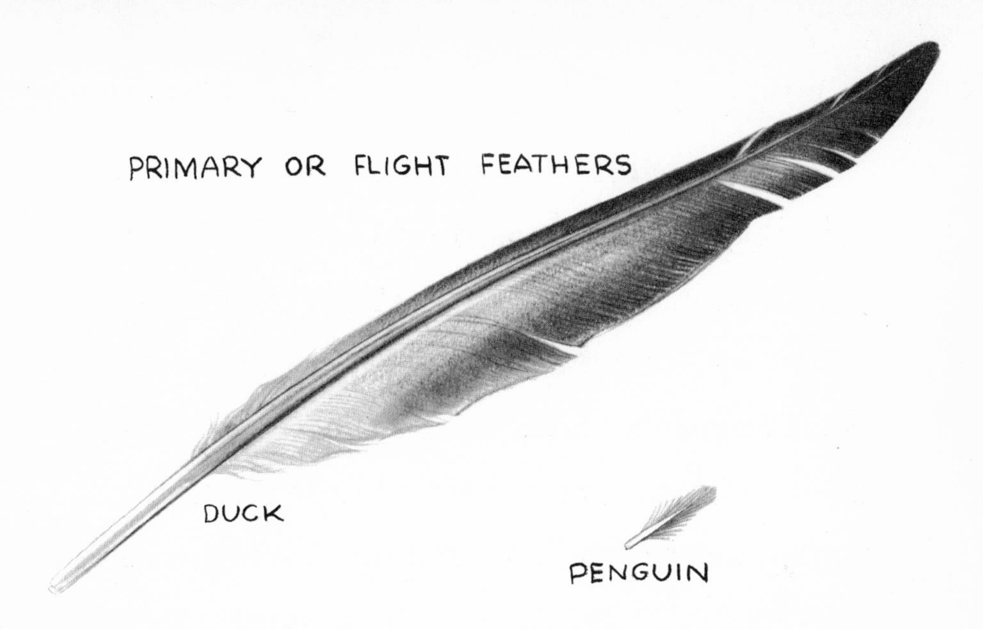

the body and form a dense streamlined coat that is a fine insulator against wind and water.

The feathers of the paddlelike wing are small and stiff, with such broad, flat shafts that the very tiny ones on the forward edge are almost all shaft. On the rear edge of the wing there are no long flight feathers, but rows of many short feathers with extra-strong shafts. Long, flexible flight feathers, like those on the wing of a flying bird, would not be stiff enough for swimming.

A penguin's skeleton is much the same as that of other birds as far as the actual bones are concerned. But the shapes of some of the bones are very different.

The bones of the wing are flattened. This allows the whole wing to be very thin and streamlined, but still strong enough to push the bird through the water. Its shape is much like that of the flipper of a seal. Some of the

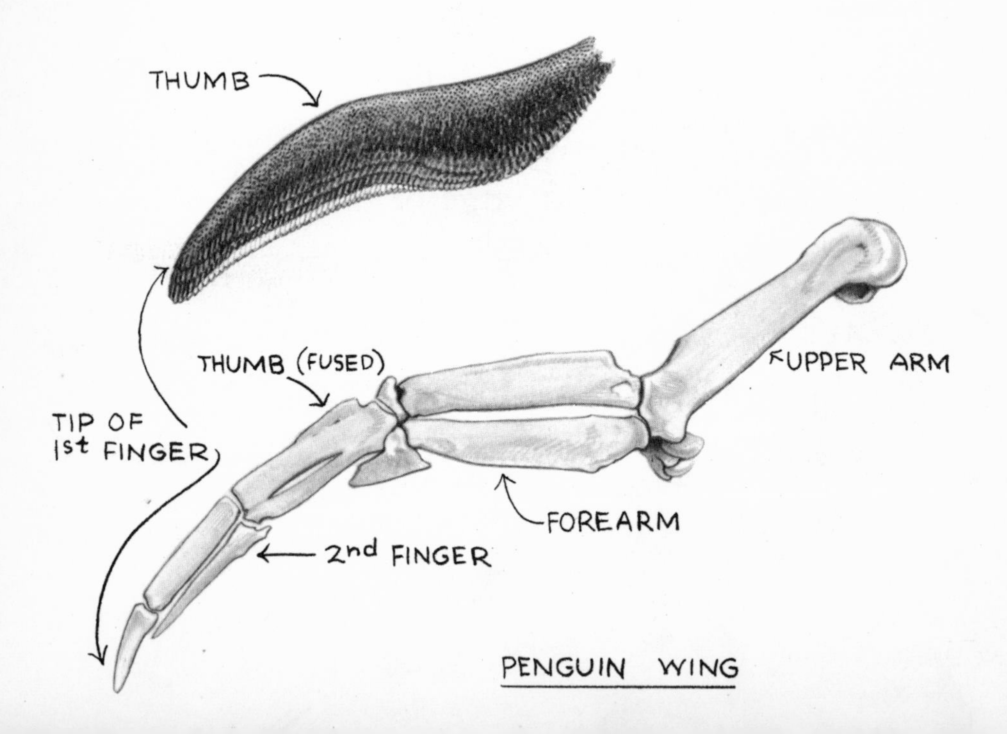

PENGUIN WING

bones of the wing have grown together, so that the penguin paddle is stiffer, even though thinner, than the wing of a flying bird. The breast muscles, which work the wings, are as large and powerful as those of any bird, but the muscles which are in the wing itself are small. Many of them are largely made up of slender bands of strong tendon. This, too, helps in making the paddle wing flat and thin.

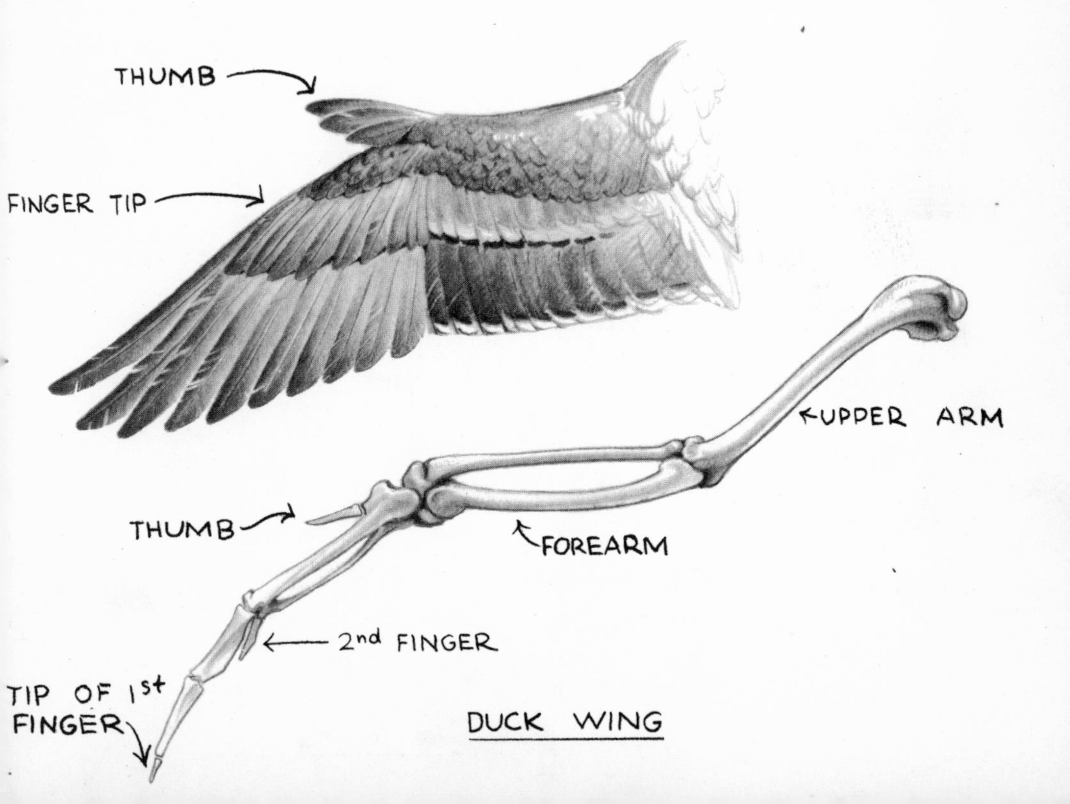

DUCK WING

Penguins do not have to be as light as the fliers. The skeleton, and indeed the entire bird is heavy. Many of the bones in other birds that are hollow and filled with air are solid in the penguins.

It is hard for eyes that are best suited to seeing in air to see well under water. Light is scattered there, and brightness is cut down rapidly by even a little murkiness. In the antarctic it is very dark even a few feet under the surface.

So penguins' eyes have had to become adapted to the water. Their eyes have become so changed for this reason that penguins cannot see well on land, where they are very nearsighted.

EMPEROR
PENGUIN SKELETON

The coloring of penguins is also best suited to life in the water. Their backs are dark and their undersides light. Many fish, dolphins, whales, and other animals are shaded in this same way. When seen from above, with dark water below, the dark back is hard to see. When seen from below, the light undersides blend with the bright skylit surface of the water. From the side, the light coming down through the water strikes the dark back, making it lighter, but leaves the white underside

in shadow, making it darker. This "flattens" the shape of the penguin and makes it hard to see from this angle also. This kind of protective coloring, called countershading, helps an animal hide from its enemies and its prey.

When a penguin comes out of the water, it stands upright and loses all the advantage of its countershading. But on the islands where they breed, most penguins have no natural enemies to hide from.

All these changes have made it impossible for penguins to live like ordinary birds, but they are truly wonderful in the place where they belong—the sea. When traveling, they glide along under water and then flash up in a perfect arc to take a quick breath and disappear without a ripple. They look like tiny porpoises, as they swim along or play about the bows of ships. When diving for food, they stay down for half a minute or more, surface for a second, and dive again. Adélie penguins have been known to bring pebbles up from the bottom in water over sixty feet deep and to swim under ice floes hundreds of yards wide. Many

penguin species leap out of the sea onto high ice or rock ledges. The Adélies will high-dive from the rocks or ice. If the water is deep the dive is clean, but in shallow water they do flat belly flops to keep from hitting the bottom.

Penguins like to play in the water. They roll about, splashing, diving, and calling to each other. Often gangs of them take rides on ice cakes that are being swept along by the tide. The birds jostle about, crowding and pushing each other off into the water like boys on a float. When the ice floe has gone far enough, they all dive off, swim back to another piece, and take the joyful ride all over again.

Penguins like to climb. They clamber up over glaciers, icebergs, and high cliffs for no apparent reason. They manage to reach the most difficult places and heights that seem impossible for a bird that cannot fly, or even walk very gracefully.

Penguins seem to be fond of company. Often when they go somewhere—and they are forever going places apparently just for the fun of it—they form long lines or large groups and march along like companies of soldiers. On their migrations across the ice, they move in lines reaching out of sight over the frozen ocean. Lone penguins will often stay with other species of penguins, different kinds of birds, or even people, just for company.

The climate of the water of the oceans varies from place to place, just as the climate on the land does. Different areas have different temperatures. Minerals brought from the land by rivers are suspended in the waters in different amounts in different places. Oxygen and carbon dioxide are absorbed from the air in different quantities depending upon water temperatures. So conditions favorable to life in the sea vary a great deal. As a general rule, cold waters have more of these life-giving elements in them. When the sunlight shines down into such rich waters, conditions for the growth of plants are perfect—not the sort of plants we

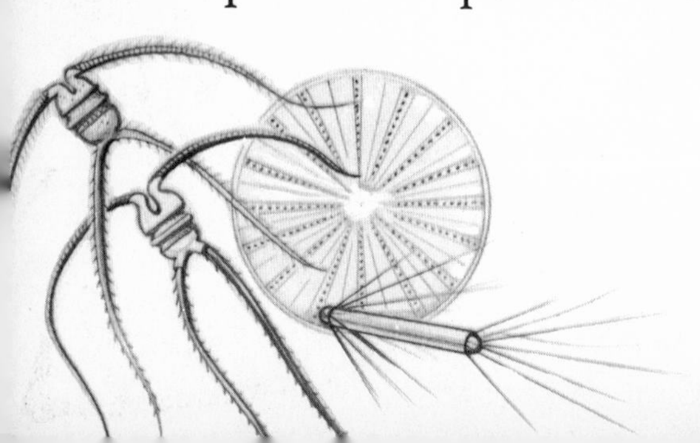

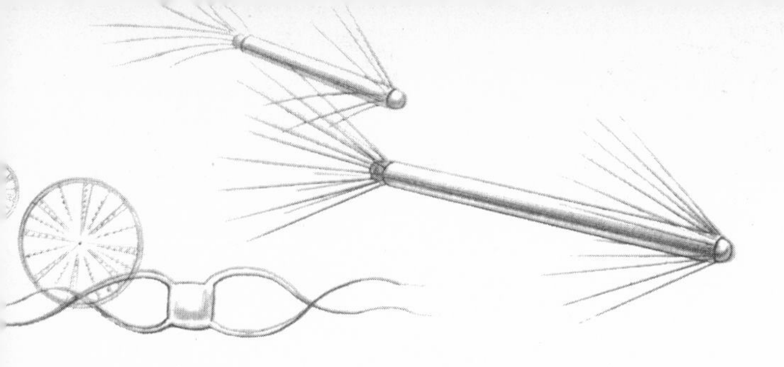

know, but tiny microscopic plants called diatoms, which look like little sculptured jewels. Like all plants, diatoms turn the energy of the sun into living matter. There are hundreds of thousands of them in each quart of water. Millions of billions live and die in the seas and furnish food for tiny animals called crustaceans. Some fish, sea birds, seals, and even the great baleen whales live on the crustaceans. Still other animals feed upon these crustacean eaters or upon each other. In this way, the energy of the sun and the minerals from the land are made available to sea animals, large and small, through the little diatoms.

The most plentiful crustaceans in antarctic seas are the opossum shrimps. Whalemen call them krill. These are the penguins' favorite food. Many antarctic penguins eat almost nothing else, although squid, a relative of the octopus, and small fish are a large part of the diet of some. Penguin species living farther north eat similar food, as all these places are surrounded by water almost as cold as that in the antarctic.

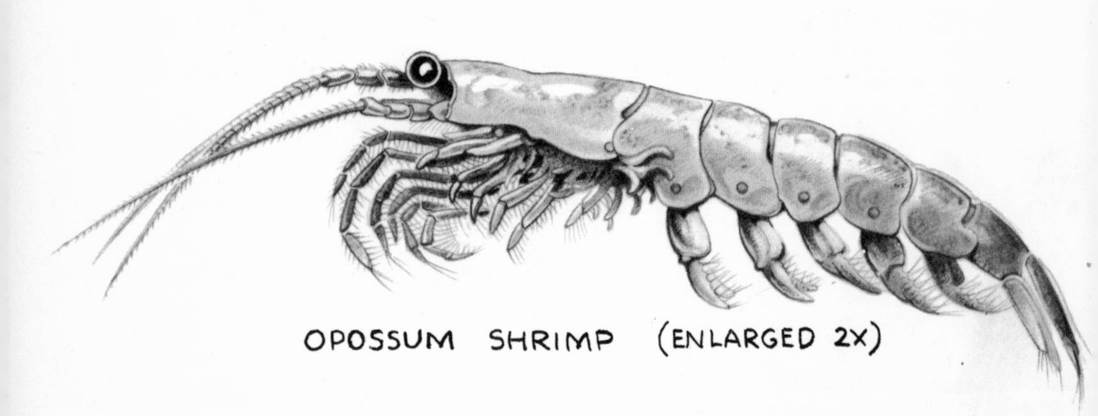

OPOSSUM SHRIMP (ENLARGED 2X)

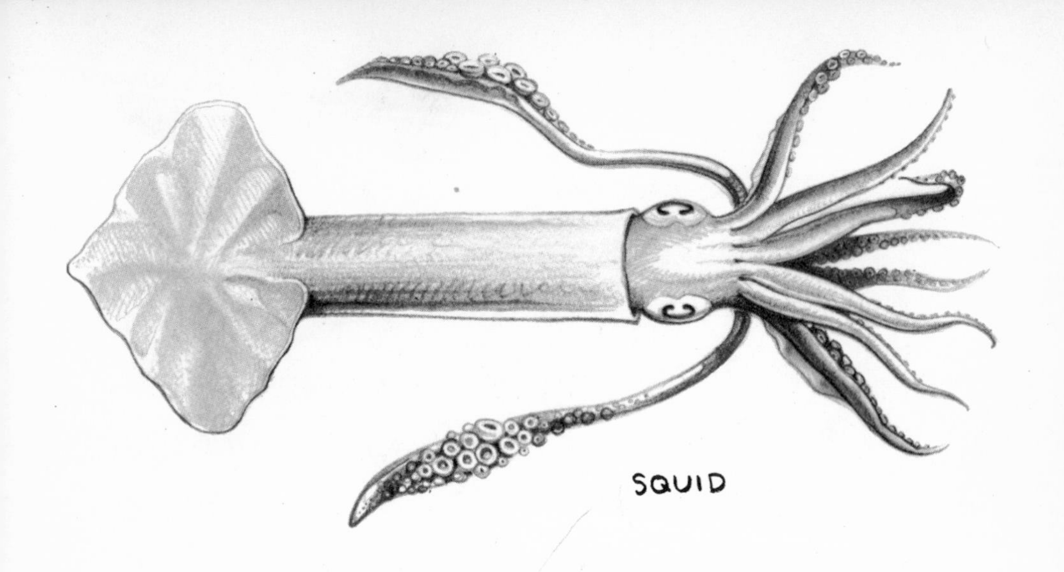

All penguins feed upon living, moving food caught in the sea. They know this food by instinct inherited from their ancestors. When by chance they come upon proper food on land, or when it is given to them by man, they will not eat it. Penguins kept in captivity have to be trained to eat by having food forced down their throats, unless they are fed living food in tanks of water. Sometimes this training takes weeks. Left to itself, a penguin would starve to death while sitting next to a heap of fish.

Most penguins live in places where man has never been until quite recently. They have not been acquainted with him long enough to develop an instinctive fear. They are very curious and sociable birds. Often they will walk right up to a person and examine him closely in their peering, nearsighted way. Troops of them will even follow a man about. Courting penguins have been known to lay pebbles at a man's feet and display to him. They seem to mistake him for another penguin until he fails to act like one.

Penguins are fierce fighters when they are defending their young or their eggs. They will throw themselves at a man's legs and pound him with flippers and beak. Walking through some penguin colonies can be a bruising experience. The strong-billed Magellan penguins

can take a good-sized chunk of flesh from a careless hand. The big emperors are tough customers. They can beat a dog, and it takes half a dozen men to capture one.

Their fearlessness and their habit of nesting in large colonies have been hard on penguins where man has come in contact with them. Their eggs are especially prized, and taking them regularly every year has almost wiped the birds out in some localities. The birds themselves are often killed for food, although an old-time antarctic explorer said that penguin tasted like a mixture of "beef, fish, and duck roasted in the same pot with cod-liver oil for sauce."

Before man and his dogs came to the areas in which penguins breed, the adult birds had no enemies on the land. The only animals which prey upon adult penguins do so in the water. The most dangerous of these is the sea leopard, a large seal. Sea leopards hang about where there are plenty of penguins swimming to and from the fishing grounds. They wait under the ice foot or in the beds of seaweed, catch the penguins, and swallow them whole. Over thirty birds have been found in the stomach of one sea leopard.

The penguins' upright posture, their curiosity, friendliness, and nearsightedness have tended to make people misunderstand them. The strange antics they go through in courtship, the habit of marching about in long lines for no apparent purpose, of going off to sleep

right in the middle of doing something else, and of playing about in what seems a silly fashion make people think of them as both funny and endearing. Titles like "Nature's Comedian," "Clown of the Antarctic," and so forth are given to stories about them.

Penguins are not funny at all to other penguins. The things they do that seem comic to us are the very qualities that make it possible for them to live so well in such difficult places. Human beings, for all their intelligence, could not live in many of these areas for an hour if they were not supplied with food and clothing from gentler lands. We may not understand the why and wherefore of all the penguins' actions, but we can be sure that they are the right things for them to do. During millions of years, the miracle of changing life has given penguins a wonderful fitness for living in some of the worst climates in the world.